A HUNDRED SUNS

First published in the United Kingdom in 2024 by
Three Highgate Editions
3 Highgate High Street
LONDON
N6 5JR

www.threehighgate.com

Distributed by Shearsman Books,
PO Box 4239, Swindon SN3 9FN, United Kingdom

A CIP catalogue record for this book
is available from the British Library

ISBN 978-1-7395449-1-1

ACKNOWLEDGEMENTS

A special thank you to Anna Kiff, Martha Kapos, John Talbot
and the Estate of Ken Kiff for all their help and guidance
and their contributions to this book.

A HUNDRED SUNS

Ken Kiff and the poets
Martha Kapos, Frank O'Hara
and Vladimir Mayakovsky

Essay by Alistair Hicks

Edited by Irina Johnstone

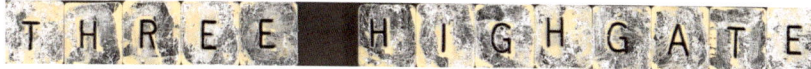

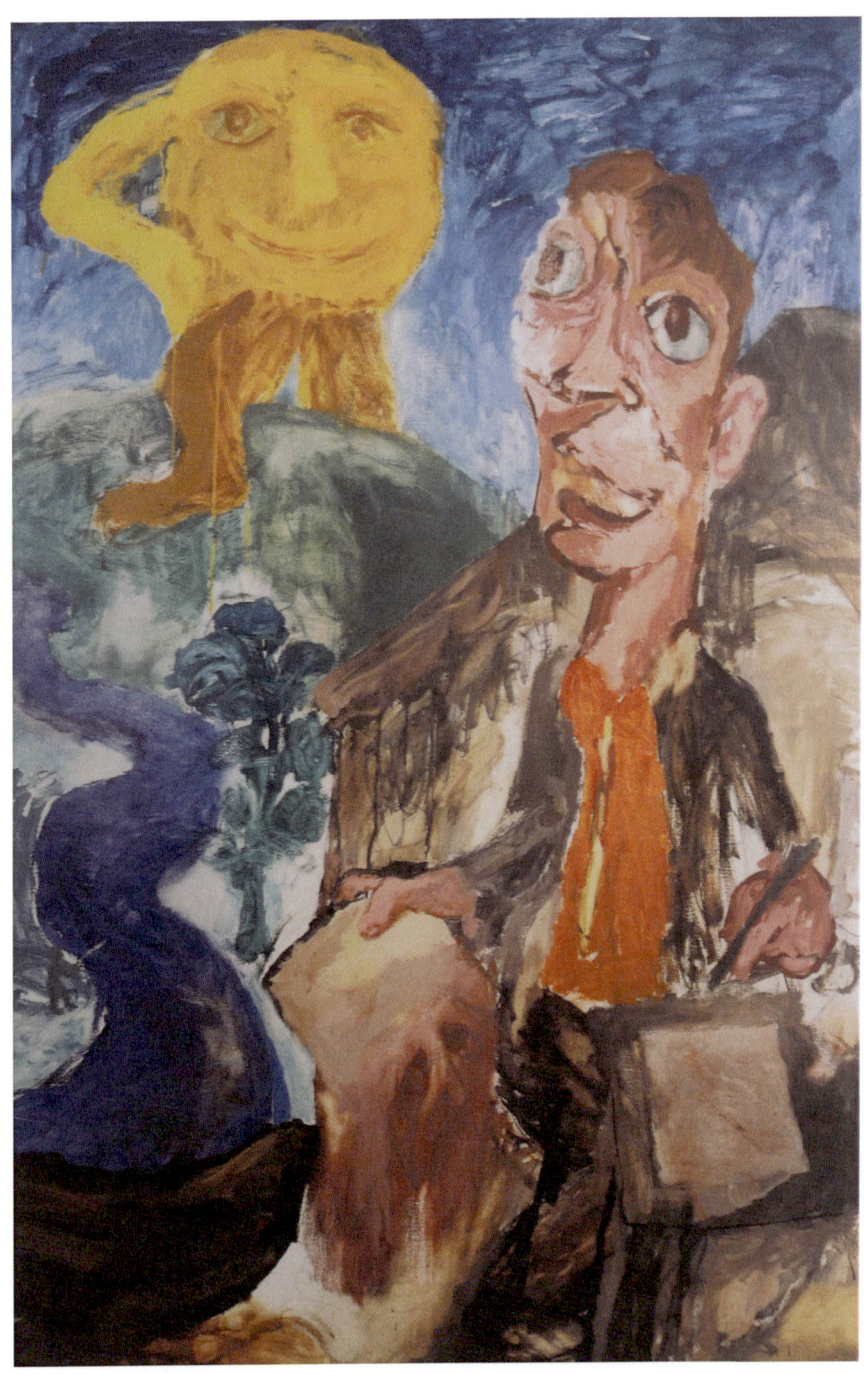

The Poet Vladimir Mayakovsky Invites the Sun to Tea

Exult!

Three poems by Mayakovsky, O'Hara and Ken Kiff's close friend Martha Kapos shed light on the way Kiff, like Paul Klee before him, took a line for a walk, and then another line, and then yet another. Kapos' poem was inspired by *A True Account of Talking to the Sun at Fire Island* by Frank O'Hara, which was written in jealous awe after reading Mayakovsky's *An Extraordinary Adventure Which Befell Vladimir Mayakovksy in a Summer Cottage*.

The three poems, the three conversations between the three poets and the sun, look for the reason to get out of bed in the morning. Over a samovar of tea, the Sun tells Vladimir that it is his creative duty to shine as a poet. He berates O'Hara for taking fifteen minutes to wake up: 'Don't be so rude, you are only the second poet I've ever chosen to speak to personally.' And as for Martha, he assures her: 'I'll not measure out any more distress than you'll need to write your poems.'

Kiff uses paint as the poets use words – pushing his blocks of colour together, shifting them around until they blur and rhyme. His exploitation of complementary colour is second to none. Yet as with poets, the technique and understanding of the language are but tools to reach another place. 'Fantasy,' he said, 'is a way of thinking about reality.'

Kiff made specific paintings in homage to poetry including the 1985 canvas, *The Poet Vladimir Mayakovsky Invites the Sun to Tea, 1985–7* (see opposite), but more importantly he had similar aspirations in his art to poetry. He would agree with Gaston Bachelard's dictum that 'The poet does not describe, he exalts.' Kiff needs to depict 'A hundred suns in one sunset.' Kiff was an intellectual, with endless nagging doubts. He was always questioning, and his reasoning was byzantine, circuitous, forever probing, but when it came down to the paintings, he managed to conjure up those hundred in one. Not that this stopped him doubting himself, which is why he embarked on the Sequence, as one painting is never enough.

If one wants to engage with the full ambition of Ken Kiff, one needs to take the path along the two hundred works in his Sequence, but this little book and exhibition is taking Bachelard's advice. Following Kiff's meandering but always needle-sharp thinking can distract from the essential simplicity of individual works. Let's just enjoy the paintings, the poems and the hundred suns.

An Extraordinary Adventure Which Befell
Vladimir Mayakovsky in a Summer Cottage

(Pushkino, Akula Hill, Rumyantsev's Dacha, 27 miles down the Yaroslav Railway)

A hundred suns in one sunset
                     blazed,
the summer rolled into July,
and the heat haze
hovered –
at a dacha all this happened.
Pushkino ridge rolled up
beneath Akula hill,
and at its feet
– a village lay,
with twisted bark of roofs.
Behind the village –
a gaping hole
and into that hole, let's say,
the sun climbed down each
                     day,
slowly and surely.
Next morning
again
to flood the world with light
the sun rose up all scarlet.
So it went on day after day
and this started
to wind
me up.
And one day being so enraged,
that all things went pale with terror,
Point-blank I shouted to the sun:
"Get down!
Enough hanging out in that hotspot!"
I shouted to the sun:
"You Freeloader!

6

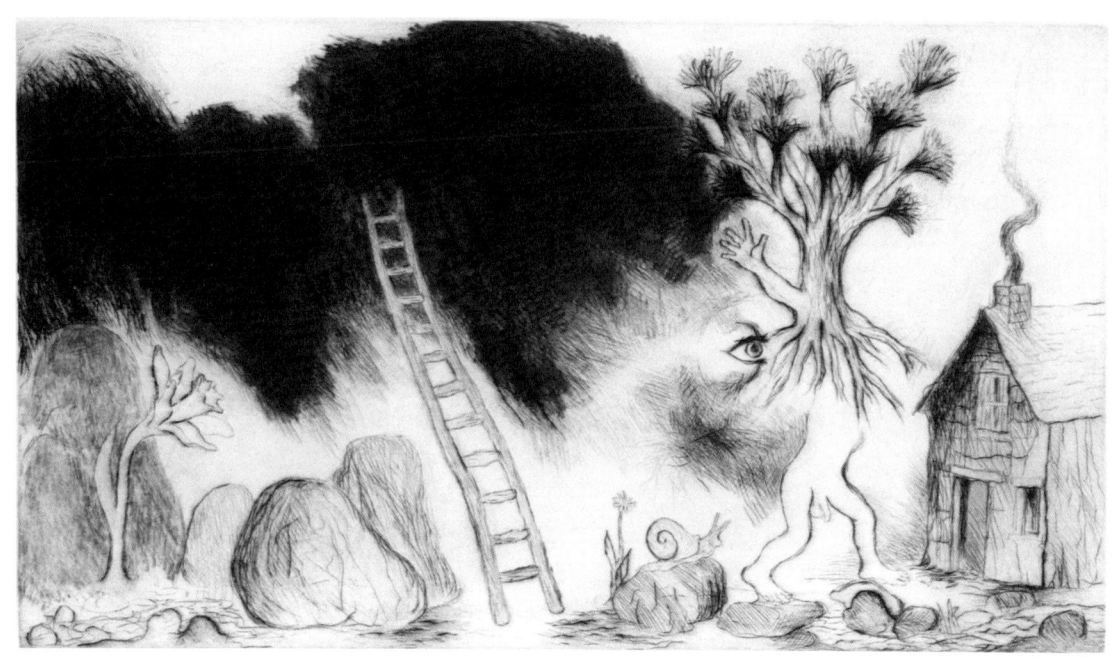

'A village lay with twisted bark of roofs'

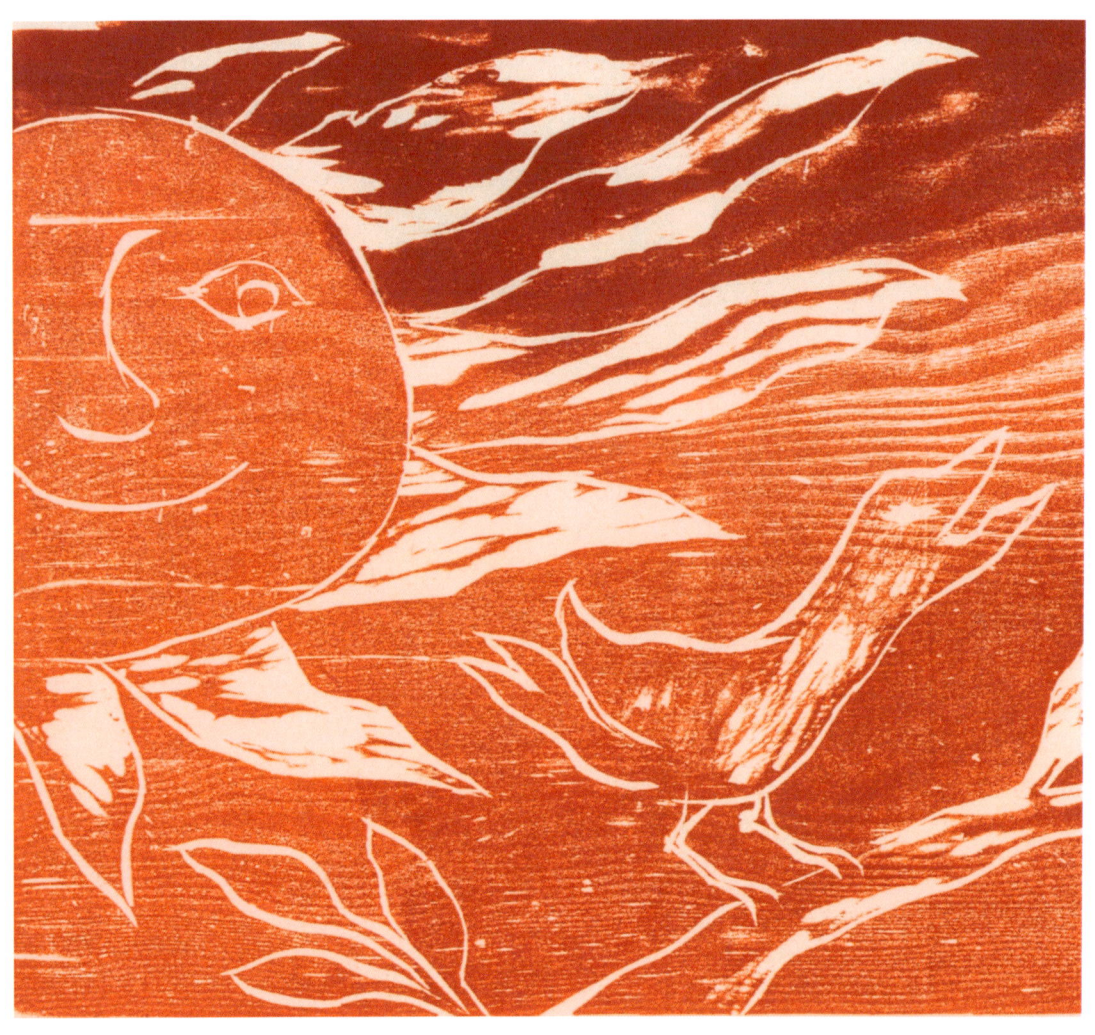

'the sun rose up all scarlet'

Sitting up there pampered by clouds,
while down here – not knowing whether it's winter

or summer

I sit and paint my posters."
I shouted to the sun:
"Hang on!
Listen to me,
you goldbrow,
instead of going down pointlessly,
come on down and have some tea!"
But what have I done!
I am doomed!
Willingly
towards me,
the sun,
with sunray steps,
is striding across the field.
I am retreating backwards –
putting on a brave face.
Now his eyes are in the garden,
now he is walking through the garden.
Through windows,
through doors,
through cracks,
the sun's abundance tumbled in.
He tumbled in,
getting his breath back,
he spoke in a deep baritone:
"I'm holding back my flames
for the first time since creation.
You called on me?
Then, you poet,
lay out some jam and tea."
There were tears in my eyes –
the heat was driving me insane,

but I got out
the samovar:
"Of course, luminary,
sit down!"
What devil made me
shout these insolent remarks –
I sat down,
blushing,
fearing to make things worse!
But a strange radiance
and gravitas
flowed out of the sun.
Forgetting it all,
I loosened my tongue
and started talking.
Talking about this and that,
that I am sick of
working for 'Rosta'.
The sun says:
"It's OK,
don't complicate things.
Don't worry!
You think it is
easy for me
to shine?
Just go try it!
But on you go –
you took it on,
you go and you shine your eyes out!"
On we chatted until what used to be the night
till the hour of darkness –
but what darkness could there be now?
Comfortably,
we are on first name terms.

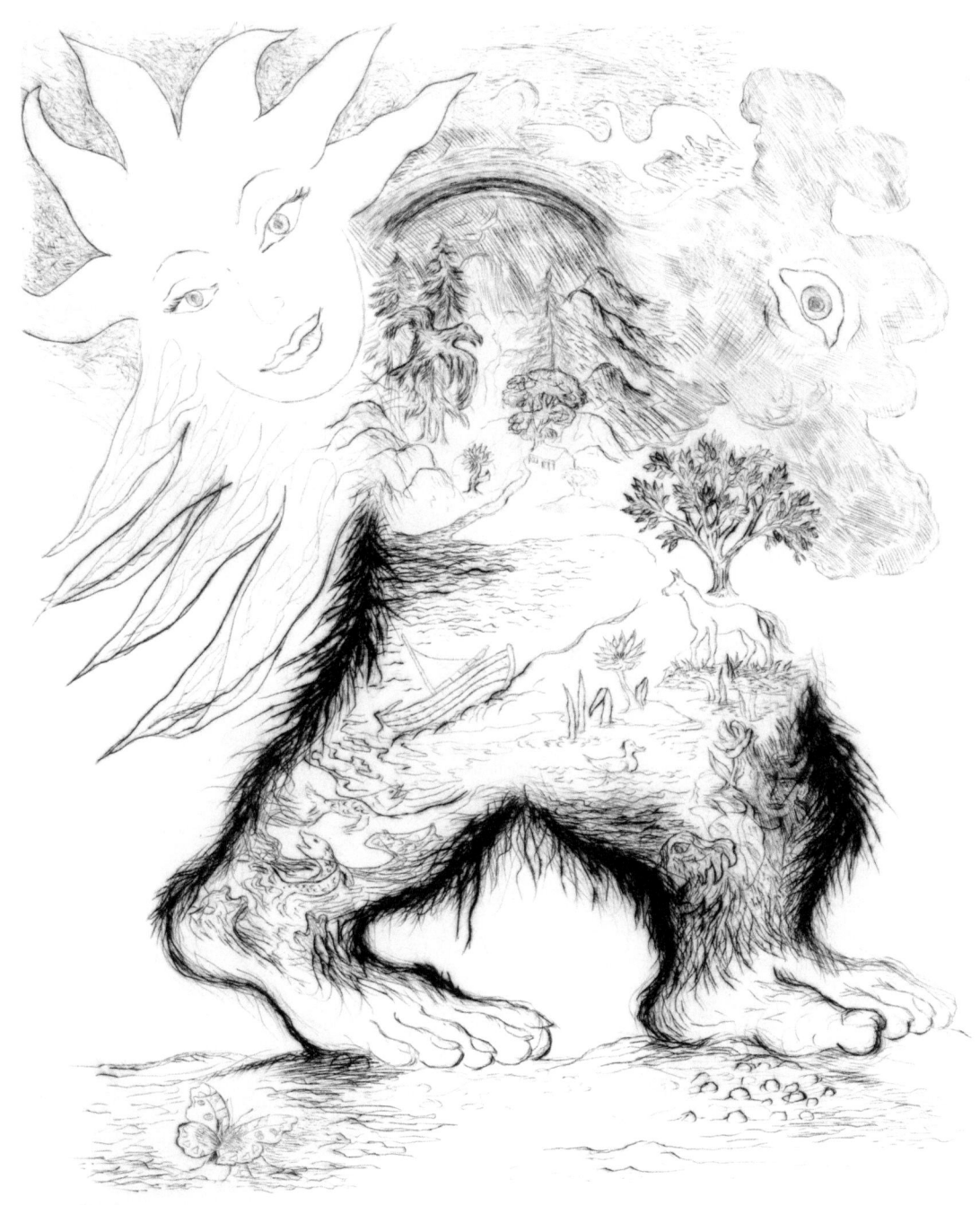

'the sun is striding across the field'

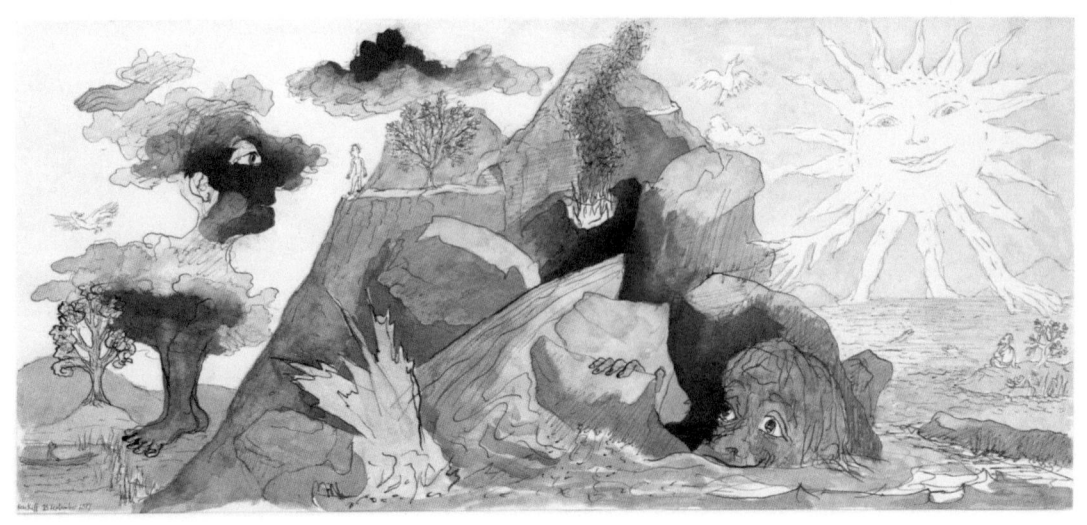

'and shine your eyes out'

And soon,
in open friendship,
I slap him on the back.
And the sun too:
"You and I,
comrade, are quite a pair!
Let's go, poet,
let's sing and
bring the dawn
to the grey drabness of the world.
I will pour out my sun,
and you – your own,
in verse."
Our double-barrelled gun blasted
the wall of shadows,
the jails of night.
The barrage of poetry and sunlight
shine at everything in sight!
The night gets weary,
and craves to lie down,
a lame sleepyhead.
Suddenly – with all my might
I rise and shine –
and once again the day is ringing out!
Shine on always,
shine on everywhere
until the day you die,
shine on –
that's all!
So say both –
the sun and I!

Written by Vladimir Mayakovsky, 1920.
Translated from Russian by Irina Johnstone, 2024

Mayakovsky's poem teases our deepest early religion, the worship of the Sun. The sun commands us to get up every day. The sun demands we shine as it shines for us. Mayakovsky lives with the pressure of many more than his famous hundred suns, until ultimately, poignantly, he can't. On the 14th April 1930 he shoots himself, not as Kiff shows him doing it, in the head, but in his heart.

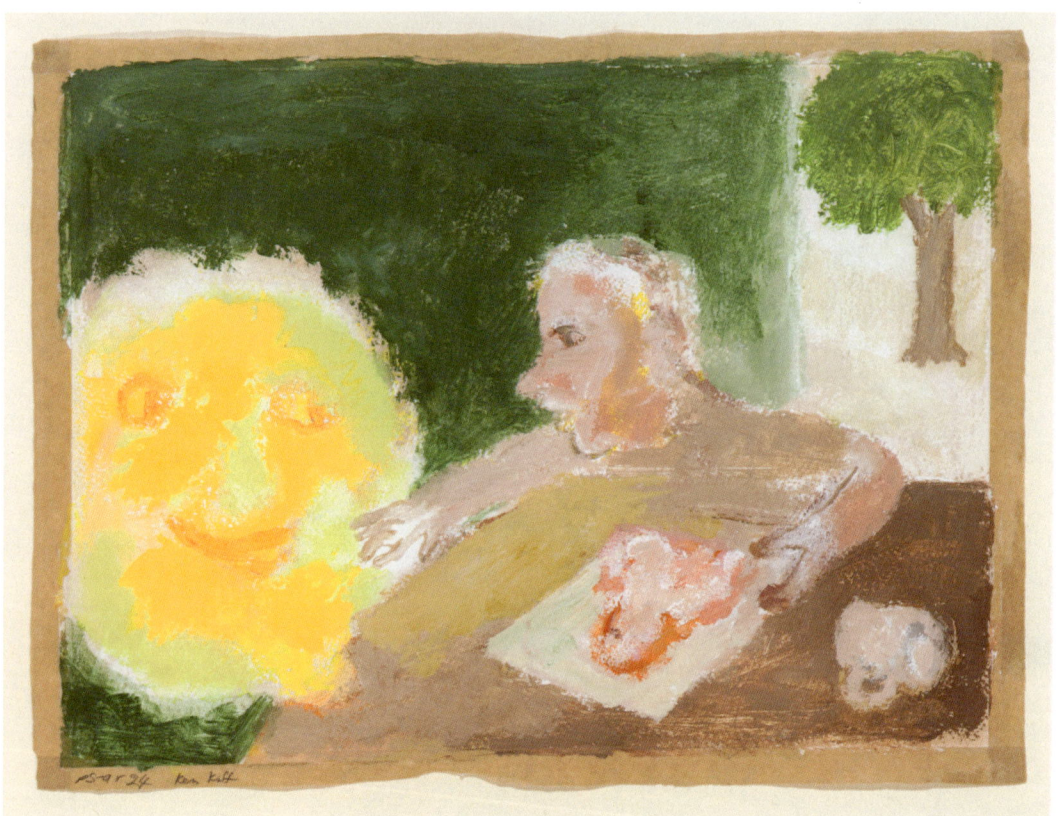

Sequence No. 24, Frightened of Good shows the creator bravely putting out his hand to stroke a sceptical sun. It is our duty to shine.

Before we let Frank O'Hara take up the story some ten thousand dawns later, and the scene moves from Moscow to New York, I would like to take you on a typical Ken Kiff digression. Often in conversations with Ken he would take his audience on one tangent, only to lead you down another slightly diverging path. He would ask us to follow his labyrinth of thought and feeling but would always come back to the knot of the argument. In this case it is confronting the sun and its promise of life.

Our detour takes us to the Museum of Modern Art. Ken Kiff's work is a minefield of missing links. The poets Wallace Stevens and Frank O'Hara are two critical rungs in this story as they shed light on Kiff's complicated relationship to abstraction. Kiff was derided by his fellow teachers at Chelsea School of Art for persisting with the central human narrative in the high age of abstraction.

In 1951 Wallace Stevens came to the Museum of Modern Art and delivered in a low droning monotone his lecture on *Relations Between Poetry and Painting*. It was the same year that Frank O'Hara got a job on the front desk at MOMA to be close to his beloved Matisses. He worked there for the rest of his life, earning promotion to becoming an assistant curator.

'Abstraction (in poetry, not in painting) involves personal removal by the poet' writes O'Hara in a manifesto he wrote gently mocking Steven's infallible belief in abstraction. The first section of Steven's *Notes Toward a Supreme Fiction* was headed *It must be Abstract*. Stevens was making a religion out of abstraction.

The sun plays many roles in the poems of Mayakovsky, O'Hara and Kapos. This is echoed by Kiff's suns. He too is reacting against the edict that the sun's rays must be all embracing and abstract. Instead, he has turned the sun into people, but one is never quite sure of their sexuality or indeed identity. Kiff had long conversations with Jungian analysts. Iain Biggs points out that James Hillman could have been describing Kiff's Sequence when he wrote, 'the soul … ceaselessly talking about itself, in ever-recurrent motifs in ever-new variations, like music.' Fantasy and reality blur in Kiff's suns and lovers. Hillman talks of a 'healing fiction' that requires 'the perpetual dismemberment of being and not-being a self.'

In the early hours, before the sun came up, on 24th July 1966, O'Hara was riding in a beach taxi with some friends. It broke down. A jeep crashed into them in the dark. O'Hara died the next day.

Nine years later John Elderfield joined MOMA as Curator of Painting and Sculpture. He has been a supporter of Kiff's work and bought *Sequence No. 68 Visiting Hell in a Boat*[1] for the Museum.

MOMA's Kiff could be a scene from Dante's rings of heaven and hell. There is a sense of being taken on life's long journey. Central figures in his 200 Sequence paintings often carry the burden of the narrative in his paintings. The majority show a little man as the hero/antihero, but the size and sex vary, as Kiff was an early believer in multiple identity. There is invariably more than one starting point and one end for our journey. O'Hara may have taken some time to be woken by the sun, but he gets its message:

'always embrace things, people earth
sky stars, as I do, freely and with
the appropriate sense of space. That
is your inclination, known in the heavens
and you should follow it to hell, if
necessary, which I doubt.'

(From 'A True Account of Talking to the Sun at Fire Island',
written by Frank O'Hara, 1958)

---

[1] An eponymous poem was written by a poet James Green in response to this work. It was published in the catalogue of Kiff's exhibition at the Gardner Center Gallery, University of Sussex, in 1979.

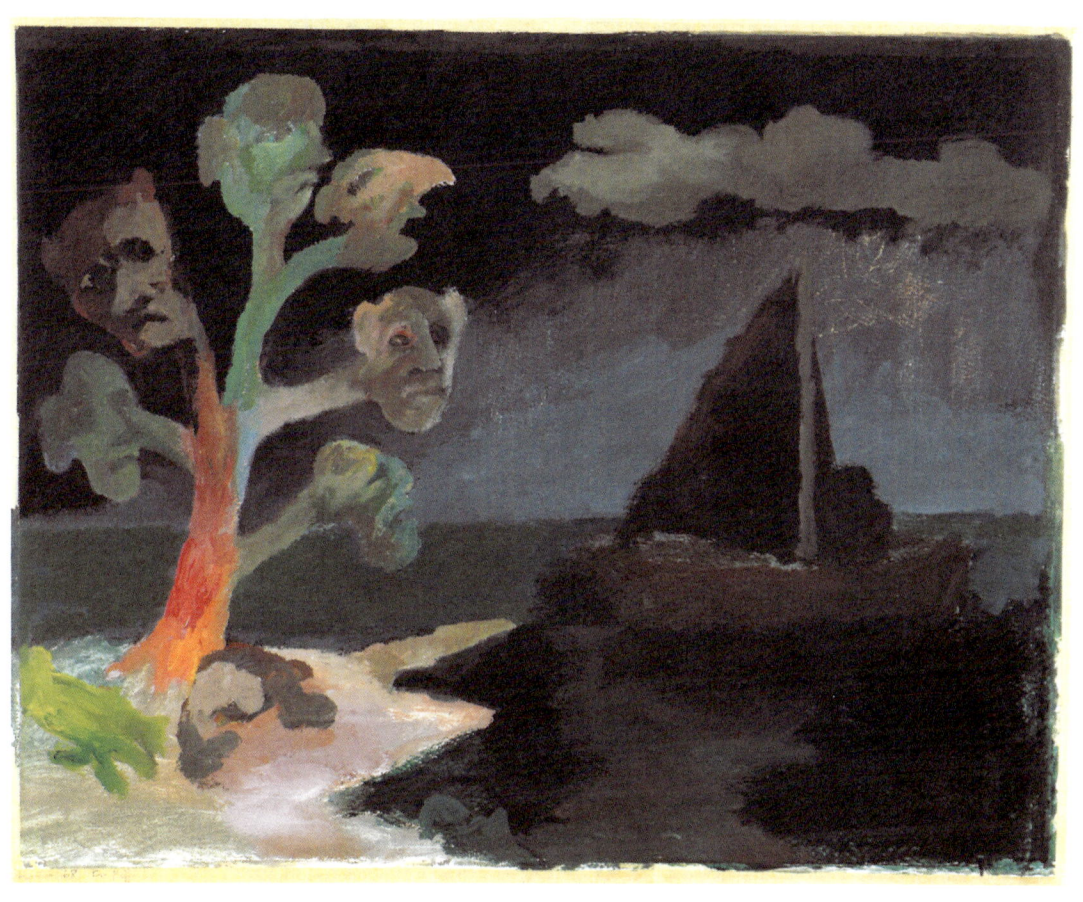

Sequence No. 68, Visiting Hell in a Boat
Courtesy of the Museum of Modern Art, New York.

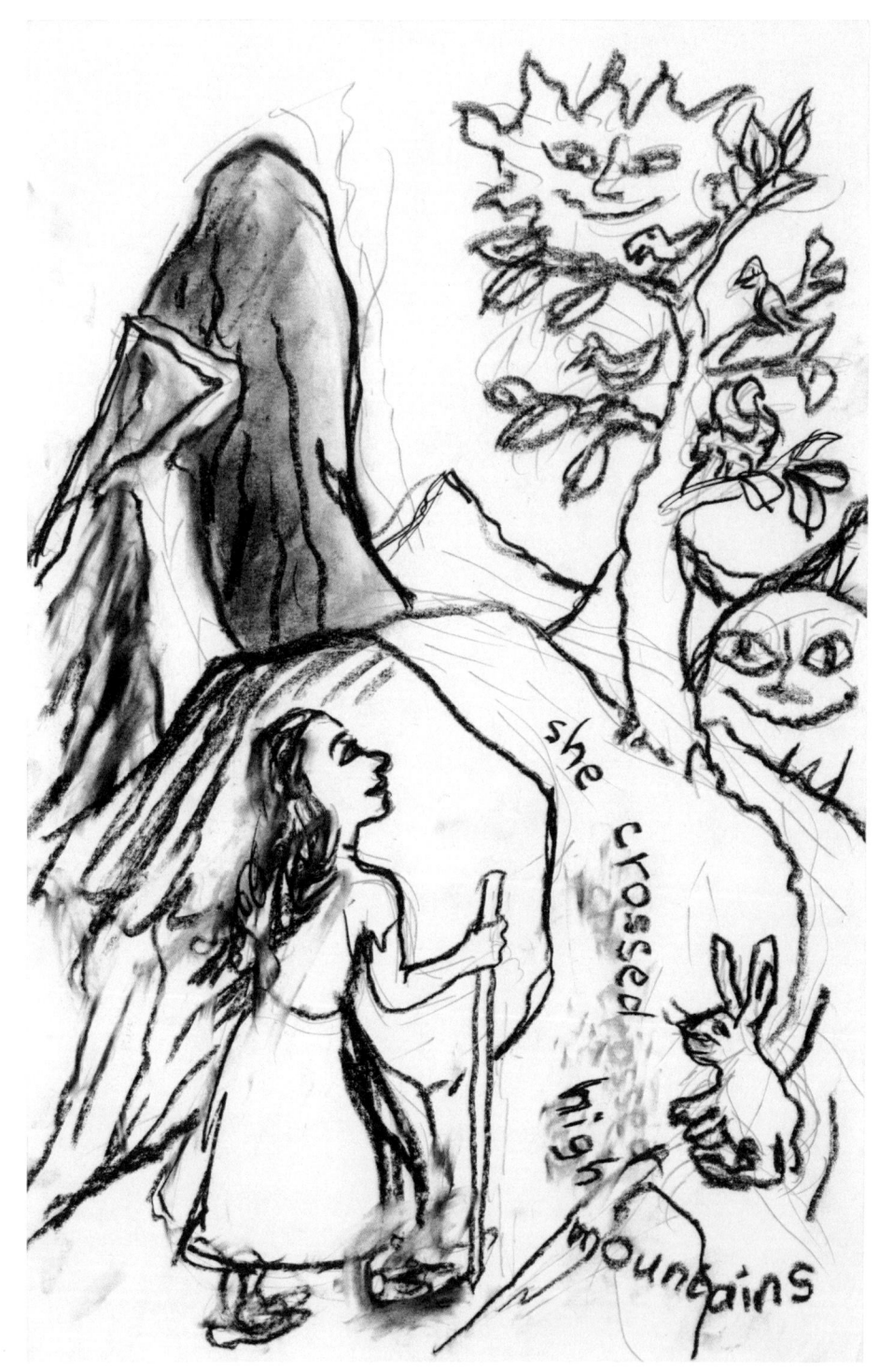

she crossed high mountains

Martha Kapos, in an essay on Kiff, uses a quote from Wallace Stevens to demonstrate how the painter uses colour and form just as a poet plays with words and metaphors. She writes that 'Like the word in poetry which floats forward … colours and forms lying together on the picture-surface are loosened.' She likes the way the word 'hermit' seems to have come out of nowhere in Stevens' *Notes Towards a Supreme Fiction*:

> '…and yet so poisonous
> Are the ravishments of truth, so fatal to
> The truth itself, the first idea becomes
> The hermit in the poet's metaphors
> Who comes and goes and comes and goes all day.'

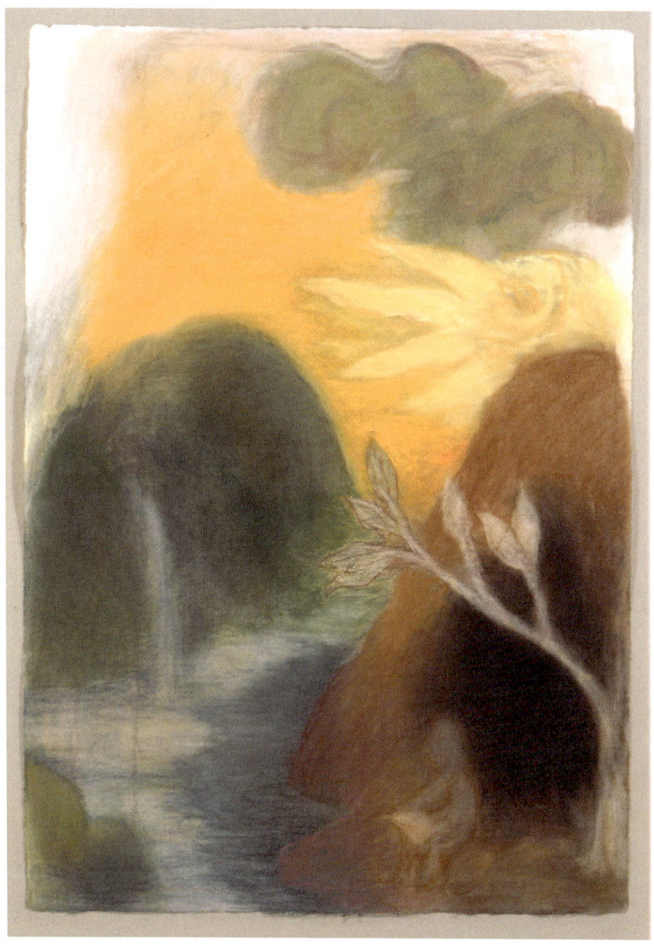

A True Account of Talking to the Sun
in Parkholme Road
after Frank O'Hara

'You told me trees pick up again
where they've left off –
but now, without their leaves
they have such a look of naked
emaciation that their hard
curves and hollows stand out like ribs
on the bare chest of Buddha.
And that Japanese Maple now bent and stiff
under a slick of white-out ice
left off last fall with an exceptional red
they'd said on *Gardeners' Question Time*
was a distinct sign of stress.'

      'Be patient'

said the Sun, loud and clear
as it stepped in through the window.
'You know what an act of faith it takes
to believe I'll put in a reliable
appearance in the morning?

        Well –

I'll not measure out any more distress
than you'll need to write your poems.'

'Can I be certain of that?' I asked.
'Not always', said the Sun.

Written by Martha Kapos, 2014

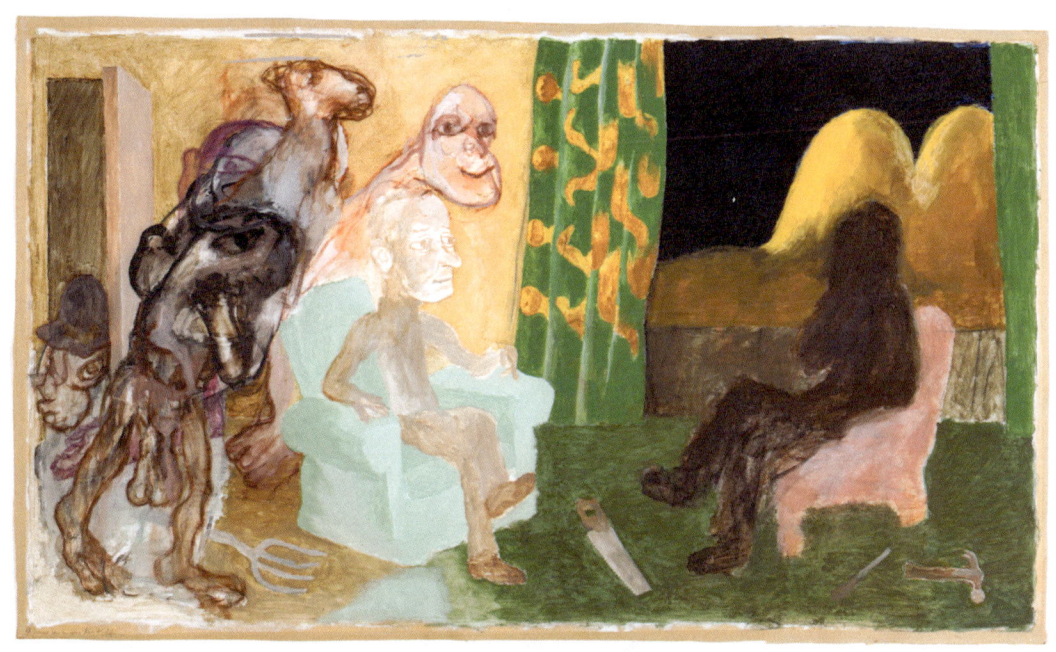

'I'll not measure out any more distress
than you'll need to write your poems.'

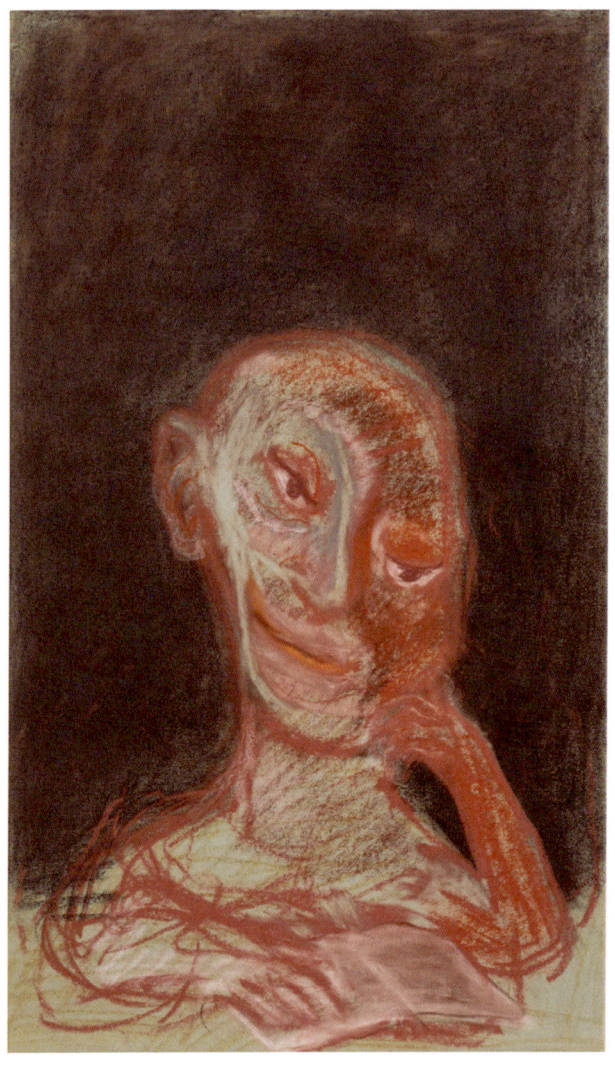

Reflecting on the painting appearing on the cover of this little book, Kiff noted: 'The 'poet' I think of as Mayakovsky. But he isn't dead, and the 'brains' are flowers'. Even in the act of ending his life, Kiff sees Mayakovsky obeying the Sun, echoing O'Hara thought 'Simply to live does not justify existence, for life is a mere gesture on the surface of the earth, and death a return to that from which we had never been wholly separated; but oh, to leave a trace, no matter how faint, of that brief gesture! For someone, some day, may find it beautiful!'

Alistair Hicks, London 2024

List of Artworks

The Poet (Mayakovsky), 1977 (front cover)
The Poet Vladimir Mayakovsky Invites the Sun to Tea, 1985 (p. 4)
The Ladder, 1994 (p. 7)
Dawn Chorus, 1988 (fragment) (p. 8)
Man Walking, 1991 (p. 11)
Untitled – Island, 1987 (p. 12)
Frightened of Good, 1971 (p. 14)
Visiting Hell in a Boat, 1973 (p. 17)
She Crossed High Mountains, 1977 (p. 18)
Hermit, 1992 (p. 19)
Talking with a psychoanalyst: night sky, 1973-79 (p. 21)
Man Reading, 1980-83 (22)
Writing a Poem, Snake, Candle, 1999 (back cover)

www.ingramcontent.com/pod-product-compliance
Lightning Source LLC
Chambersburg PA
CBRC090944170526
45162CB00011B/83